Disclaimer:

The Blackboard training guide is designed for the sole purpose of training based upon the experiences and results of personal coaching and customer service training of Tiffany Michelle. We do not guarantee any specific results of private training.

The Blackboard is not liable for any loss or risk that teams, companies, or trainers may incur utilizing the enclosed material. We guarantee the individual who wants to change will change with focused and consistent efforts in any part of their life.

The Blackboard™
Customer Service Training Guide
Copyright©2017

Introduction

Do you treat others the way you want to be treated? Think about that for a minute. The golden rule of customer service is to treat others the way you want to be treated. There is no exception to this rule!

You've probably heard the customer is always right. However, they're not! But what can you do about it? Treat them like they are and you'll be glad you did, it $$ pays. This doesn't mean you have to compromise the company polices. But it does mean you should be committed to protecting the company's reputation and making the customer's experience great.

Therefore, equipping yourself with the right tools to handle any kind of customer service issue is essential to doing it the right way, the first time.

The company's policies and procedures serve as a roadmap for guiding your actions. Nevertheless, people skills are what make the difference in winning your customer.

Your initial interaction with your customer is the ticket to building trust, closing the sale, and making them want to come back again.

Whether it's a new, repeat, or unhappy customer you can apply the following strategies to reach them all: the golden rule, the 5 Be Attitudes, or engage customers with your knowledge.

What you will learn:

- The importance of applying the "golden rule" of customer service when dealing with new, repeat, and unhappy customers

- How to win any customer with the **5 BE ATTITUDES** of Customer Service…

- Why engaging customers with your knowledge is key to them leaving with your products and services

Notes:

_____

_____

_____

_____

_____

_____

_____

_____

_____

_____

_____

_____

_____

_____

_____

_____

_____

_____

_____

_____

_____

_____

The Golden Rule of Customer Service

Doing unto others as you would have them do unto you is the **golden rule** of customer service. Remember it only takes one action to either lose a customer or build a lifelong customer. Treat your customer as if you were serving yourself.

In other words, how would you want to be treated if you were in the customer's shoes?

Your company relies on you to treat their customers well every day. Their profit margins depend upon it and your livelihood is based upon the success and profitability of the company. Furthermore, your attitude and care of the customer is directly related to how profitable the company becomes over time.

Notes:

_____

_____

_____

_____

_____

_____

_____

_____

_____

_____

_____

_____

_____

_____

_____

_____

_____

_____

_____

_____

_____

_____

_____

You'll see the benefits of the **golden rule** in your personal and professional success. A good attitude will put you on the fast track to promotion. Basically, you can increase your income by treating people well.

Also, think about the influence this has on your peers at work. Learn to be an example to those who don't treat you well. Take the time to assess each situation before you pass judgement.

You could be dealing with someone in the middle of a difficult personal situation. Although their attitude is difficult right now, treat them the way you would want to be treated. If you both have a bad attitude just imagine the atmosphere you're creating for everyone else. If you practice this simple rule with your co-workers and you'll nail it with the customers.

Personnel should take on the values and morals of the company when handling difficult customers. Doing this provides a model for consistently dealing with customers the same way each time. This makes the team appear more knowledgeable and credible.

THE BLACKBOARD™ TRAIN. RETAIN. MAINTAIN RESULTS.

Notes:

_____

_____

_____

_____

_____

_____

_____

_____

_____

_____

_____

_____

_____

_____

_____

_____

_____

_____

_____

Customers need to know they'll get the same service regardless of the employee helping them. This helps avoids misunderstanding and dissatisfied customers.

The Golden Rule of
Customer Service principle:

---

*Always treat the customer well, no matter what they do.

Notes:

_____

_____

_____

_____

_____

_____

_____

_____

_____

_____

_____

_____

_____

_____

_____

_____

_____

_____

_____

_____

_____

List three of the company's values that helps you to be fair and consistent:

1._____

_____

2._____

_____

3._____

_____

THE BLACKBOARD™ TRAIN. RETAIN. MAINTAIN RESULTS.

Notes:

_____

_____

_____

_____

_____

_____

_____

_____

_____

_____

_____

_____

_____

_____

_____

_____

_____

_____

_____

_____

5 Be Attitudes of Customer Service

Be Genuine with every customer you interact with during the course of the day. Genuine people exudes confidence and credibility. Moreover, your personality shines through. When people like what they see they're more apt to buy. If you're really appealing to them, they'll buy more from you.

Customers want to feel you're being honest with them regarding the products or services you're selling. Show them you have their best interest in mind by gather information about their lifestyle and buying habits. During the buying process apply that knowledge to the products and services you recommend.

Notes:

_____

_____

_____

_____

_____

_____

_____

_____

_____

_____

_____

_____

_____

_____

_____

_____

_____

_____

_____

_____

_____

Customers can sense if you're genuine or just going through the motions. Let's face it, most of us, if not all of us have experienced sales people helping us because it's their job, not to deliver exceptional customer service.

Besides, customers equate being genuine with an authentic brand that provides quality products and services.

Always Be Respectful. The tone you set with the customer upfront will determine the outcome you get. For instant, if you have an irate customer and you become irate, things will only get out of hand. Although you certainly will not agree with everything the customer says, stay calm and allow them to vent. If they disrespect you, put the fire out immediately with soft words. They'll remember how you treated them and will be less likely to act that way again with you.

It's so much easier to win someone if you're polite. Listen to the customer's request and go the extra mile. Make them feel important by being attentive. Don't

Notes:

_____

_____

_____

_____

_____

_____

_____

_____

_____

_____

_____

_____

_____

_____

_____

_____

_____

_____

_____

_____

let what's going on divert your attention elsewhere. Be sure to give the customer as much time as they need, then use it to close the sale.

This is the difficult part of customer service. There's no way around it. Unhappy customers will always challenge you to dig deep and give them your best.

Don't take the harsh words personal or allow these situations to overwhelm you. Clear your mind and serve your next customer. If you don't, you can't deliver exceptional customer service.

Notes:

_____

_____

_____

_____

_____

_____

_____

_____

_____

_____

_____

_____

_____

_____

_____

_____

_____

_____

_____

_____

Whenever you find yourself in a difficult situation with a customer or co-worker remember to do the following things:

- Smile
- Be polite
- Remain calm
- Don't replay negative conversations in your head
- Think about your response before you speak

Notes:

_____

_____

_____

_____

_____

_____

_____

_____

_____

_____

_____

_____

_____

_____

_____

_____

_____

_____

_____

_____

Be Generous and give the customer more than they expect every visit. It will breed loyalty. Don't start off with top-notched services or products and as you grow give less. This is a major trap for businesses, customers notice and overtime become dissatisfied and leave. It is more cost effective to keep a customer than acquire a brand new customer.

Generosity is your way of letting the customer know you appreciate their business. Going the extra mile for them is worth it and doesn't have to be costly. For example, give special shopping privileges, a chance to win something not yet available to other customers, personal invite them to exclusive event, etc.

It says generous is who we are not just something we do. Have someone take their shopping bags to the car for them. Upgrade their gift wrap from basic to glam or offer refreshments. Whatever you do make sure they leave with a smile on their face.

Notes:

_____

_____

_____

_____

_____

_____

_____

_____

_____

_____

_____

_____

_____

_____

_____

_____

_____

_____

_____

_____

What you have to give up is small in comparison to the conversations they'll have with their friends and family. This will result in repeat business from that customer and referrals of new customers based on how you took care of them.

Be careful that you don't include the product or discount you offer for the inconvenience of the customer as extra when a problem occurs. Going the extra mile should be done in addition to resolving the problem.

If you see a pattern of complaints from the same customers and believe they are trying to take advantage of the situation, remind them you are there to help but you need their full cooperation.

Advise the customer that you practice the golden rule of customer service and firmly state it to the customer. Ask them to do the same.

Notes:

_____

_____

_____

_____

_____

_____

_____

_____

_____

_____

_____

_____

_____

_____

_____

_____

_____

_____

_____

_____

_____

Doing so reinforces how genuine you are with your customers. The golden rule of customer service is unspoken. However, your actions are on display every day. Taking the time to explain this further to the customer should help you in your attempt to successful resolve the matter.

Notes:

_____

_____

_____

_____

_____

_____

_____

_____

_____

_____

_____

_____

_____

_____

_____

_____

_____

_____

_____

_____

_____

_____

Be Personable. Make the customer's experience as pleasant as possible. Remember to smile often and be conscious of your body language. Don't alienate the customer by leaving them alone to long. If you need to leave them, let them know you'll be back after they've had an opportunity to look around. Use good manners at all times. The smallest measure of politeness and hospitality will make even the most discerning customer feel right at home.

The main benefit of being personable is to get information about their needs, preferences, and lifestyle. Listen carefully to everything they tell you! It makes it easier to provide options for purchase.

They'll let you know right away of any objections that you need to address. Don't change your attitude toward the customer if things start to go downhill. This is the time you'll really want the customer to trust you. So maintaining a good attitude can go a long way in establishing their trust in a short period of time.

Notes:

_____

_____

_____

_____

_____

_____

_____

_____

_____

_____

_____

_____

_____

_____

_____

_____

_____

_____

_____

_____

Thinking quick on your feet can be extremely valuable. Try not to take a lot of time finding solutions or offering suggestions. It could possibly irritate the customer and make the matter worse. A simple solution is to know your product and services well.

Overall, a polished presentation is important to being portrayed as being professional, knowledgeable and credible. The way the customer views you matters because your goal is to win them in every way.

Furthermore, your personal appearance and being easy to get along with is absolutely necessary to being personable. People are more apt to approach you if you're clean and neat. Also, if customers find it easy to get along with you they're more likely to be open to your suggestions.

Notes:

_____

_____

_____

_____

_____

_____

_____

_____

_____

_____

_____

_____

_____

_____

_____

_____

_____

_____

_____

_____

_____

_____

Be a Problem-Solver. Learn how to listen for underlying issues. You have to gather the facts, analyze the information, and decide how to move forward quickly. Asking the right questions will determine the quality of your decision. Remember to reflect the goals and values of the company in your actions. Excellent customer service is doing the right thing, the first time.

This may be your only chance to win the customer. Don't ever give up a sale because you're too lazy to find a solution. Or it's much more convenient to just let the customer leave. If you know your products and services well making the customer happy want be a problem.

If you don't have exactly what they want, solve the problem with what you have. While this may be a challenge, be creative and get the job done. Don't give your customer the opportunity to say no to you. It could have big benefits for you. A letter to the owner or boss on how you've helped them, a promotion or raise if the solution lead to a major sale, or an outside job offer.

Notes:

_____

_____

_____

_____

_____

_____

_____

_____

_____

_____

_____

_____

_____

_____

_____

_____

_____

_____

_____

_____

People are always watching you, just when you least expect it you'll be rewarded for a job well done.

Solving problems for customers and your company will open many doors for you. Every time you solve a problem you master a situation, increasing your skills and value to others.

Notes:

_____

_____

_____

_____

_____

_____

_____

_____

_____

_____

_____

_____

_____

_____

_____

_____

_____

_____

_____

_____

_____

Engage Customers with Your Knowledge

If you only speak to the customer and ask if you can help you have not engaged them. True engagement is getting involved with the customer from the time they come in until they leave. Keep up with current events, technology, fashion, and industry trends.

It helps to be able to strike up interesting conversations with a diverse group of customers. At the very least talk about what they're wearing or their hair, anything personal.

Notes:

_____

_____

_____

_____

_____

_____

_____

_____

_____

_____

_____

_____

_____

_____

_____

_____

_____

_____

_____

_____

_____

_____

Listen for information about their lifestyle or buying habits. Use this info to get the customer involved by demonstrating to them how the product works and why it complements their lifestyle. Sell features, convenience, and benefits.

When the customer is fully engaged then ask for the sale. You have the ability to use your personal and product knowledge to persuade every customer to purchase a product or service.

This is the time to be creative. Give the customer a fun shopping experience. Make them want to come back soon. Talk about new products or services and how you will help them when they come back. Build excitement based upon what you know they're interested in from the information you just received.

Notes:

_____

_____

_____

_____

_____

_____

_____

_____

_____

_____

_____

_____

_____

_____

_____

_____

_____

_____

_____

_____

Use the before you go cards to list the reasons your customer shouldn't leave without the product or service. Before the customer goes work your list and close the sale.

BEFORE YOU GO

Pros	Cons
1._____	1._____
2._____	2._____
3._____	3._____
4._____	4._____
5._____	5._____

Notes:

_____

_____

_____

_____

_____

_____

_____

_____

_____

_____

_____

_____

_____

_____

_____

_____

_____

_____

_____

_____

Notes:

_____

_____

_____

_____

_____

_____

_____

_____

_____

_____

_____

_____

_____

_____

_____

_____

_____

_____

_____

_____

_____

_____

THE BLACKBOARD™ TRAIN. RETAIN. MAINTAIN RESULTS.

Feedback:

Rate the training on a scale of 1 to 5.
(5 being the highest and 1 the lowest.)
1 2 3 4 5

What did you like about the training?

_____

_____

_____

_____

How can we improve upon the training?

_____

_____

_____

_____

Additional Comments:

_____

_____

_____

_____